CHANNELING DEMYSTIFIED FOR SPIRITUAL PERSPECTIVE

BY

JEROME FILIPIEC

MIRIAM STANFORD-CUSACK, PH.D.N.H.

Published by Insight Well-being, New York, New York.

Cover art gratitude of Cheryl Filipiec

ISBN-13: 978-1500884710
ISBN-10: 1500884715

This book is lovingly dedicated to our spouses and our guides. Through them our connections to higher self and spiritual perspective are exemplified.

Contents

Introduction: Channeling Demystified: a practical guide for everyone

There has been much written on the methods of channeling about the danger and, in the past, there was much to be concerned about. The vibrational energy of the planet had not yet been elevated to the extent that it was possible for the average person to channel safely. Only a select few individuals who had spent time elevating themselves to a proper vibrational frequency through meditation, fasting, and devotion to the light were able to safely determine which energies were of the light and, therefore, safe to bring in. We have seen those who made an effort to channel but whose vibrational frequency was not yet prepared. The result of this was madness and sometimes even death. Your planet is currently caught in a wave of frequency adjustment that is elevating it in to the next spiritual shift. So, a major change will happen and mankind will be faced with some very difficult decisions.

The more people that have been brought into and aligned with the light, the better chance your planet and mankind will survive the shift and move forward into the new phase of spiritual development. I am El-Israel, a light being from the next energetic level. I write with my companion Leal, who also is from the next energetic level. The purpose of our work with you is to provide a simple mechanism for the shift to happen. By giving mankind a simple process by which they are able to locate and consult with their guides and other beings from the light, more people will be able to contact and work with their spiritual advisers. They will be able to consult with the other side and trust their intuition. They will know that the messages they are receiving are for their highest good and for the good of the beautiful planet you know as Earth. This has become increasingly important as we see the energies of war and destruction increase. It has become the responsibility of all individuals to who are able to bring light and love energies to your dear planet.

Lokar: The energies we speak of are subtle and for the most part in the past have gone unnoticed. This will no longer be true for as the adjustment, elevation and refinement of planetary energy continues many more individuals, especially children, will become more aware of change in their daily lives. There will be an increased awareness of intuition working for you, a knowing at an instant of how to respond to a situation and an increase in the harmony of daily activity. The children will accept these changes as normal because for them it will be the way things are with no hindrances from previous experiences to make them expect otherwise. Adults however will know that something is different. Those who are more astute to the change in vibration may even feel slightly out of sorts. Ideas will often pop into their thoughts which seem to be from nowhere and out of context to their normal thinking. Elevating energy changes and expands brain capacity into higher levels of thought. This is an evolutionary process which not only uplifts the individual, but uplifts mankind.

This book will prepare seekers who are experiencing these changes and provide explanations and methods to benefit from the vibrational shifts. It will: explain how to come into clear communication with personal guides, guardians and angels, give the reader easy, practical and safe methods for receiving an abundance of information and wisdom, assist the beginner in their quest to understand their earthly mission through contact with their own personal guides, and give the reader practical methods to test the purity of the personality with which they are in contact. All this wisdom and more comes from guides and other high energy beings who have chosen two humble humans to deliver this vital information.

The human authors of this book have put in years of preparation through meditation, study and various workshops with no idea that each would be led to channeling without even asking.

Miriam Stanford-Cusack received an unsolicited message to write this book. At the same time, miles to the southwest, her step father Jerry Filipiec was receiving the same basic message to write this book. Both these 'authors' are really scribes which have attuned their receiving apparatus to take dictation from different higher level sources.

Miriam receives information from El-Israel, Seth and Leal, while Jerry receives messages from Lokar, a high Avatar Master and Oskar an angel whose responsibility is in part preparing mankind for the evolutionary transition into the next level of awareness. These loving personalities are supported by many others and receive information from what they refer to as the committee. An untold number of dedicated guides and high level personalities are contributing to this book with the purpose of making the tools available to mankind for the transition to improve the planet.

Chapter 1: Why Channel?

You might find yourself asking, "Why channel? Why would I choose to channel after hearing so many negative things about it? I have always thought it to be a dangerous task and have been warned against doing it by spiritual and religious teachers, being told it is a practice only for those who are most astute. "

Lokar: For many years channeling was reserved for mystics, psychics and researchers of the occult. The discipline required to learn the process was not only difficult, but time consuming. It was so because the time was not right for it to be any other way. The last one hundred and fifty years have shown great strides in spiritual movements both in the Americas and abroad. Psychic phenomena are being researched by governments, individual foundations and individual groups. Even with all these strides the knowledge seems limited to a select few who transmit their findings to the public through books about their experiences. More and more becomes available on the internet, but who can trust it, as much of it comes from sources unknown? Yet the urgency for the general public to have this indispensable tool for the progress of mankind and the preservation of the earth was never more urgent.

El-Israel: There has been much written on the methods of channeling. Much about the dangers and, in the past, there was much to be concerned about. The vibrational energy of the planet had not yet been elevated to the extent that it was possible for the average person to channel safely. We have seen those who made an effort to channel, but whose vibrational frequency was not yet prepared, make the grave and dangerous mistake of allowing entity invasion. The result of this was madness and sometimes even death. In the past a thick vibrational energy "blanket" has separated you from being fully aware of the other side. Religions have called this a veil for lack of a better term. It is the separation of mankind from the Source. It was necessary for many millennia for this to be the case as contact with the higher vibration would have "shorted-out" the nervous centers of the planet itself. Your planet is currently caught in a wave of frequency adjustment that is elevating it in to the next spiritual shift. So, a major change will happen and mankind will be faced with some very difficult decisions. The more people that have been brought in to and aligned with the light, the better chance your planet and mankind will survive the shift and move forward into the new phase of spiritual development.

Remember that all energy moves together and relates. Harmonics are not confined to music or strings, but are in every aspect of energy vibration and at all levels of interaction between frequencies. You are a frequency body, as are we, the light beings, angels and avatars. By increasing your vibrational energy to a level slightly higher than the one you have been living at as a necessity of the dense vibrational pattern of your Earth, and through our ability to lower ours to meet you, we are able to communicate at a level that was previously not experienced by humankind. The implications of this are vast and important.

Leal: If you are reading this, you have given some thought to your reason for being. You have wondered why you are here at this time and how you could be of service to others in order to maintain your connection with the Divine Source. You are a person who has made an effort to remain connected spiritually and have chosen to believe at a time when many have left organized religion and lost sight of their spiritual connections. Now that the frequency patterns of your Earth realm are being elevated, you can have the answers to your questions. You can experience oneness with your spirit and your divine purpose. You can see your future and ask questions about your current place in the grand scheme of it all. But mostly, you are able to experience the love we have for each other and that love that sustains all living things, the love that allows you to manifest your highest good on the physical level and explains your role. You will experience a love of yourself that allows you to enjoy and be at peace with where you are in your Earth life.

Lokar: In this book we will write of many things in regard to the coming times for mankind and this planet. We will write of planetary evolution for the ecology, and life in general. As the shepherds of this world, we must act as an enlightened group of individuals to prevent a downturn of the evolutionary process. To do this we need an informational resource which cannot be put into books. How can we gain the knowledge necessary to help us respond to the demands of a society and a world which is hurling itself so rapidly into the next age that conventional means will no longer work? What resources can we all reach for which are there for us in a moment to give insight, information, guidance and direction? One that has been there all along, often ignored, seldom trusted and thought to be too strange to rely upon.

El-Israel: We all have been in a place of darkness at one point. Some of us have lived Earth lives as you are doing now. Others have lived on other planes and have had other teachers than those sent to you. Through these beings we found reprieve from the darkness and a view as to the glory of the Divine. The techniques we give you have been refined for your Earth plane to lift you from the clouded vision of the darkness and elevate you above the fog to a place where you are able to experience light. Is there a better reason to channel than the experience of joy, love and awareness of who you really are?

Lokar: Well, the time has arrived for us to become more in touch with the same source which inspired the ground breaking discoveries of the past, which changed history with a decision made from insight. Buckled in to the guide channel you have the greatest single resource for information and guidance instantly at hand and now you can do it better and more quickly than ever before.

What will it do for me? Try peace of mind, a relaxed sense of purpose, the ability to check a decision almost instantly, capability to act instead of react: just to list a few of the values of channeling. This is practical stuff not esoteric mumbo jumbo. Guides talk in the language of the present helping solve problems of the present; never making decisions for their patrons, but instead opening them to a variety of alternatives. To know what's right at an instant and proceed with the assurance that your choices will result in the common good makes a life filled with satisfaction.

The processes of knowing is inherent to channeling when we channel we have a sense of knowing that something is right or wrong. That is we know what feels right or makes sense intellectually. This is the first stage of knowing. As you advance in your vibrational connection the flow of information as well as quickly guided action increases. It seems that you do things automatically, almost without thinking. All humans exercise this type of thought. It is to them almost non-thought. When you drive a car or do some activity with which you have much experience you often forget you are doing it. This is called by some an unconscious action. This doing springs in and out of consciousness as our attention requires. In driving it may be a traffic light changing colors. The signal causes a change in response so you jump into consciousness. This gently vacillating state is the most elementary form of knowing.

As experience grows one begins to enter mastery of a particular activity. We all admire such people. We enjoy the meals which are prepared by someone who is masterful in the kitchen, often saying they are an inspired cook. We marvel at the inspirations of a renowned artist, writer and ministers. The way in which they deliver their message puts us in awe. Yet, we all do this type of activity somewhere or sometime in our lives. The big indicators of understanding this first stage of knowing are joy and passion.

The weekend hobbyist may not be a great golfer, but if golf is one's passion it should bring joy. The anger which we jokingly see in cartoons- golf clubs wrapped around trees or flying through the air- are examples of frustration. This frustration comes from our lack of performance of an activity which we so love doing that our limitations of performance cause an internal anger.

Who wouldn't like to be better at what they love to do? Channeling is a secret weapon at getting better. A weapon which destroys frustration, and allows one to accept their own physical limitations as none of us are perfect. Have we not seen a champion, a great practitioner of some task, shake their head in dismay at their lack of ability to perform. Even the best cry in frustration at times but to know that you have done your best because you have used all your resources brings a satisfaction to one's life.

Channeling brings us closer in every way to knowing on a level which will astound others. This knowing brings a peace of mind which allows one to move through life's trials not as a lonely pilgrim, but with the support of guides who have devoted themselves to help you. Many a person thanks God for the inspiration, for showing them the way, and this is all very appropriate for God is the basis of all knowledge, guidance and love. Those of us at the levels of guides, avatars and angels thank God daily and praise the creator for the opportunity to serve and exemplify the Godly traits. We share these traits in the form of communication which at a conscious level is channeling. Our earthly companions profit from these communications in knowing the most important aspect of life.

Knowing the mystery of life, "Why am I here? What's the purpose of all this?"-is a cry we all hear in the upper levels coming from mankind. It is true mankind suffers, is in anguish and turmoil. Prayers seem to go unanswered for many. Confusion about which decision to make plagues the human race. The few who have made the connection of knowing don't necessarily coast through life; they do understand their purpose. The mystery of their mission on this planet for this life is revealed.

This revelation is often in stages as the individual becomes better connected to their guides and angels. On rare occasions it becomes a life changing bolt of lightning. The caution of the lightning bolt revelation is: now that I've seen the light, I can rely on my own ego and intellect and charge on independently. We have seen this happen so often in the disenfranchised preacher who prays but doesn't listen to anything but his own ego. If you're buckled into the process you've got to listen. BUT ALWAYS MAKE YOUR OWN DECISION. Being conscious of guided advice is not "knowing". Knowing is being so buckled into the informational stream of life and the communication that ideas fly into one's mind followed by actions which are natural and so suitable to the situation that even we become astounded at what we have said or done. This process is so natural that the flow between guide and yourself is grasped without any conscious thought. You know it has happened more as hindsight.

As individuals we will all make the choice to do this or not. For those who choose to continue you will find the trip relatively easy and quickly rewarding. The fact that you chose to get this book has a meaning in itself, let it set a while and see if you find yourself revisiting its pages or giving it to someone who will be eager for the contents.

Leal: Why channel? Channel because you have faith in the Divine. Channel because you have a desire to live in the presence of love and light, understanding your life's purpose and your role. Channel because you wish to be a part of raising mankind to the next energetic level and you want to see the world in harmony with a greater plan for us all. We welcome you in to our loving embrace.

Chapter 2: How do I know I'm doing it correctly?

Lokar and El-Israel: In the beginning there may be confusion as to how to proceed and what one is to do in order to start the process of connecting to a spirit guide. This comes from a desire to be shown a sign in a dramatic and tangible manner. We all ask for proofs but then are not always open to receiving them in subtle ways. In some traditions, prayers are said to the Mother Mary and something as slight as seeing a rose is proof the prayer was heard. However, we often ask for grand displays, such as winning the lottery or the miraculous healing of a friend or family member. Many signs and manifestations of our ability to connect with the other side and know we have been heard are very subtle and often within ourselves. Sometimes it is just a "knowing", a sense of peace, a calming of the nerves; feeling reassured. In many cases, one must begin with trusting the feelings in the body or the pictures that pop in to one's mind. As you progress, your sense will be fine-tuned. This comes as a result of your being meeting and harmonizing with vibrations at a higher level. You must first allow yourself to "run with it" and experience what you experience with an open mind and heart.

Step 1: Find a place in which you can spend some time which will be uninterrupted, away from the hustle and bustle of the household, a quiet place. Some will find this to be a difficult task in that things like street noise may be distracting. Turn off the phones. You may choose to have a small fan and use it to generate white noise in the background. You may also find that background music will work for you, but be careful that the tunes don't catch you and cause distraction.

Step 2: Once you have found your place, make sure you are comfortable. The sitting position is preferred to lying down. Adjust the lighting to suit you. Pick a time which is best suited for being receptive. Later on you'll be able to be receptive anytime, anywhere under a variety of conditions.

Step 3: You will want to have a writing pad of some kind to serve as a journal in which you record your progress. Some will use the pad concurrently while channeling while others will make it a summary document to record their session afterwards. Many do both. Use dates and times to record your sessions and review them no less than once per month.

Step 4: Create a protected space by asking for it. Whatever method you use for prayer or meditation is appropriate. You may want to ask for or visualize light filling the space. You may ask that God's hands surround and protect you or that the Blessed Mother or archangels create a safe space for you into which no "evil" may enter. The act of asking will always be responded to. If you ask, you can trust that Light beings, angels, the light of God's love or other protective energy will come to your aid. It is God's will that you connect with your higher guides and live in the light of love. In order for this to happen, you must experience and become familiar with the higher energy.

Step 5: **ASK AND THEN SHUT UP AND LISTEN.** Asking is crucial to the process of channeling. There are three things to ask for in the beginning:

1. Say a prayer which asks for an awareness and receptive state. Make one

up. It may be as simple as, "Lord let me be aware for my highest good so I may serve you." or, "Father please let me clearly hear that which is being given through your divine edict for the benefit and blessing of all."

2. Ask for your guide to communicate with you. You may write this on the pad or say it softly. Be comfortable in the asking you are going to do a lot of it. When you ask be specific. It may be helpful at first to make a list of questions.

3. Relax, but do not put yourself into a deep meditative state. You are preparing to have a conscious communication. If you find yourself falling asleep too often ask to remain aware. In the beginning, as your body and mind adjust to receiving communication, some will drift off to a light sleep while the energy shifts.

Step 6: This is the hard part at first. You've made your request to have communication with your personal guide. Now you wait. No one can say what will happen next, pictures may flash in your mind, colors may flow in waves, voices may be heard or some urge may occur. Do whatever seems right. These beginning processes are often filled with doubt.

Step 7: Take your time, but don't spend too much time waiting. Most beginning sessions last between fifteen and thirty minutes. Quit when you feel it's time to stop the session.

Step 8: Give thanks for the new awareness and on your writing pad record what insights, feelings and experiences occurred during your session.

Lokar: It may take a few sessions to establish a meaningful communication. When you reach that point you will need to find out who is communicating and if they are from the light. All higher beings are from the light and will do no harm to their chosen companion.

El-Israel: Determining with whom you are communicating is a vital step in the process and very important for maintaining safe energetic boundaries. You may connect first to your higher self. This is the part of you, or your "soul", that resides in the light of God's love on the other side and is in direct communication with the will of God and the source of all light and love. It is a very safe and warm feeling when you connect with this part of yourself. There is a sense of completion to your being and rejoining in wholeness. Ask that this be the first communication you make when you begin the exercise of channeling. This way, you will have the experience of an appropriate and safe energy connection. Do this several times so you are aware of and familiar with the feeling that accompanies this connection before mentally opening yourself up to receive communication from other sources. Please be sure to take a moment when you sense you have made your first connection to ask specifically if the being with whom you are connecting, presumably your higher self, is of the light and there for your highest good.

Leal: The feeling of connection will seem as though it comes from a source directly above you and will be connected in light to you through the top of the head. Many cultures refer to this area as the crown chakra. As you become more familiar with your higher self, you may ask to be taken on small "journeys" to the other side. You may ask yourself questions. The answers may come to you as words, images, or feelings. Be sure to record anything you experience as, frequently, when people are new to channeling, they forget much of what is being "told" to them and benefit from reviewing it afterward. This is similar to dreaming in a half awake state. Telling or recording the dream afterward always helps one to remember it. The same experience occurs with channeling.

From this point, once you have become familiar with the feeling of positive light energy, you may ask to connect with higher guides and other light energy beings. If you feel as though a new being is making an effort to align with your energy and initiate communication, ask their name and if they are from the light.

El-Israel: We have spoken of the times when ascetics who were not yet ready to align with the higher frequencies of the other side were fooled into believing they were connecting with a higher being only to unknowingly allow entity invasion. The result was disastrous. When a new energy approaches you and you feel as though it would like to initiate communication, it will not be able to align with your energy if it has not received permission to do so. The act of asking for confirmation as to its source as being of the light and its purpose, that of your highest good, guarantees a positive energy connection. Earth bound energies, or ghosts as you call them, or beings who do not have the goal of bringing more spiritual perspective and well-being to you will not be able to respond that

22

they have these as their intention. You may feel a slight shift in the energy that does not feel right. They may be accompanied by a color that aggravates you or appear as a type of person with whom you do not normally get along. Any discomfort or questioning you experience should be taken as a sign that the being trying to make a connection should be rebutted. The process is quite simple. Tell them to leave. You do not have to feel bad about not being polite. They were impolite to try to access you without proper intention. You may tell them to leave out loud or mentally with determination. You should immediately feel the energy shift back to a place where you feel comfortable and content. Any being there for your benefit will feel loving and give you a sense of security.

Leal: If you find it difficult to maintain a connection and ask the questions you have written while you are in your connected state, you can tape them first and listen to your own voice asking. It is very important that, after you ask a question, you give yourself time to focus in and accept the response. When Miriam first began asking questions, she was flooded with images and information that were difficult to separate and decipher at once. If this happens, you may ask to have only one guide communicate at a time and begin by letting yourself write whatever comes in to your mind, without thought. This form of auto writing is very useful and provides tangible evidence of the answers to your questions. Miriam often finds that, as she goes back to read what she has written, she is surprised. Often, she does not have recollection of having written certain phrases and the point or meaning of what she has written is usually not obvious to her until she rereads was has been "dictated". Trust that you are open to the communication. Even if the answer comes from your own higher self, it will be true for you and your higher self is always in communication and direct connection with the will of God.

Once past this point the real adventure begins.

You will find that each individual's experience is different, some vary slightly from others while one or two from a group may dive right in and have a strong connection immediately; others will link up more slowly. In the beginning these connections with guides often start as being subtle flashes and insights. Ideas may start popping into your head and you begin to write them down on your pad. You will question the authentic nature of these early responses. This is part of the process. Responses from your guides need to be tested as to their validity. Beginners go through the procedure of discovering the difference between channeled thought and self-thought. Take time during or after to record the process. You will remain conscious and aware of the interaction with your guide. It is after all a conversation between two or more dear friends. What do friends talk about? Lofty 'Spiritual Matters', surely sometimes but not always. Friends talk about their problems, discuss their plans, find reassurance, and get advice. They have normal conversations.

Do you always take your friend's advice? You most certainly take it in consideration, but in the final action you do as you darn well please. Your spirit guide is a best friend never interfering with your free choice in a matter. Never offering advice unless asked for and only illuminating a course of action. Never judging what you chose to do with your life. If you are one who seeks approval for a particular action you might be surprised at the answers you'd get from your guide. Ask them if you did a great job you might get your ego pinched in the process. The guides accept what you do; they give you options and never run the person's life for them.

Chapter 3: What's the easy way to the other side?

Lokar: In the beginning you sort of accept there is an "other side" with which you can communicate. You believe that this other side is full of life in a fashion that is not earthly, but whose members have an earthly connection. You may have been taught a religious dogma about a heaven and a hell. Jerry has asked Oskar, his angel companion, and was told, "No harps but a lot of singing". Many have experienced the Angelic Choir at various times in their life. There are so many levels of consciousness that the astral geography and all the different beings and places are mind boggling. On this side we Guides pretty much stay to our chosen tasks relative to the missions on which we are working. We form groups of common interest. Some choose to help individuals progress. While others choose to support issues and tasks to help arrange suitable environments for change, through the earthly individuals they work with and influence. As it becomes necessary and appropriate, information about specific levels will be forthcoming.

The key issue which makes it easier to get to the other side is having some knowledge of what is there. Each individual's perception and experience will vary. They will all have points of similarity. To start, you are expecting to communicate with a human type of personality. Guides have been human on this planet so they know of the physical conditions which human beings enjoy as well as suffer through. This makes the experience easier to communicate as we are more apt to be at ease communicating with another human. The truth of the matter is we are beings of a higher vibrational energy and have a body which is energetic, more like a glowing form. Many refer to this as a light body.

The way to the other side is not a physical or mental visit to a place as you would do on earth going to visit a neighbor or relative. It is akin to a type of remote communication or remote viewing. This viewing of the party or parties with whom you are connecting is associated with your individual desire and shapes itself accordingly. The process of connecting is diverse for all individuals. You all have different strengths and preferences in connecting and communicating. This connecting varies from everyday communication, but the communication is translated into a meaningful earthly experience. How one expects to connect and communicate is often different from what happens. Some find that their earthly strength or preference may be visual and yet when they attempt to see the other realms they can see nothing. All is blank. This nature of opposite experiencing is not unusual, but it often frustrates the beginner who expects to have a visual experience because that's who they think they are and it is their expected perception.

The way to avoid this type of frustration is to be open to the idea and purpose of your connection. You are in the process of opening lines of communication with an old friend who has been distant and unreachable for a long time. Your friend is trying to reach you in the best way for the communication to happen. They have a lot more knowledge as to how it will happen than you. In fact *the beginner often blocks the process of communication by insisting at some level of their own consciousness that the process will be accomplished through a particular method*. In other words, it is best to simply ask while you wait for your guide to make the connection.

Leal: The process of connecting with your guides can be one of extreme joy and a sense of well-being. You should never experience any discomfort, fear or anxiety. If this is the case, you may ask the archangels or light beings to protect you and surround you with the light of love and keep all negativity at bay.

Your guides are tuning in to you and this may take some time. Think of your experience with a radio. You are turning the dial and hear the faintest crackle of a voice or music. You turn the dial back and forth until you have tuned in to the best reception possible. It may require you to use antennae or you may have to move the radio to another area in order for the best signal to come through. When you open up to us and "broadcast" energetically we sense the slightest opening of a channel. We must adjust our frequencies to yours. In some cases an effort is made to help you raise your vibrational frequency to a level in which we are able to come down and meet you. Once a clear connection has been made, we continue in subsequent sessions to find a better connection. We fine tune our adjustments. At the same time, the experience of joining with a higher level vibration causes yours to begin to resonate, in harmony. Over time, it becomes easier for us to find channels that will correspond and for our messages to come through to you. Your vibrational level continues to adjust, elevate and refine each time a connection is made. For this reason, the method by which you experience this communication may become clearer or change, all together.

Lokar: To make it easy, first know that there is a loving friend who wishes ever so greatly to exchange ideas with you, give you advice about choices, open your thought to new vistas and nurture your progress in this human lifetime.

Second, as you quietly wait for the communication from this friend always *expect that you will be in communication*. The means of the pending exchange will be revealed in an instant. Understand that your guide(s) start working on themselves and you when the request for communication is made. They are adjusting frequency vibrations between the two of you to clarify and enhance the coming exchange of ideas. This adjustment period can last days or even weeks. Your guides select the best means for the two of you to begin. This very often changes as your connection grows in strength.

Leal: You may find, like Miriam, you begin with a sense of the guide. Later, the frequencies you have evolved to are better expressed through writing. At some point, you may be speaking the answers to your own questions.

None of these methods is more or less valid or superior to the other. Evolution from one type of contact to another does not necessarily mean elevation to a higher level than another. It simply means that you, and we, have found the best way to connect. It is important that you not begin to judge yourself or others based on a false sense of what form of communication indicates a higher level, more spirituality or an elevated connection to God. Connecting with your guides, at this point, is strictly for your own good and your own personal spiritual evolution. It is not an ego- based pursuit that means one person has achieved a status greater than another. Being open to your own growth without ego involvement is crucial to achieving the most benefit from your guided sessions.

Lokar: If nothing seems to be happening and you have sat quietly waiting, most likely random snatches of ideas will pop in and out of your mind. Write them down immediately as they occur. If you find that you are vocalizing, talking to yourself, get a tape recorder and turn it on in the beginning of the session and then promptly forget about it. Some have found recordings on their tapes having forgotten to turn on the machine when they started their session. Visual experiences are rare in the beginning, but they are not unheard of. Always remember that what you desire is being fulfilled by your best and ever friend, your guide.

El-Israel: Even if your first trials are only for a few minutes, observe what is happening on all levels. Afterward, record your thoughts, feelings, and experiences, on any level, on the notepad. Take the time before your next session to review your notes and remember the feelings and impressions you received. In this way you begin to familiarize yourself with your own personal method of connecting to the other side. It may change and you may have more sensations or "hear" or "see" in your mind's eye. All of these are valid and personalized to you and your vibrational frequency.

Lokar: Be patient. Your guide is performing what you would consider a Herculean task in adjusting not only their energy to be receptive to you- this is often called by some lowering their vibration- but also working on energetic portions of your brain to open avenues of connection, channels. These channels become the means through which the energies which carry the communication travel.

El –Israel: All beings are desirous of a connection with God. This is the nature of being a part of the love and light energy that is God.

We are all drawn back to our source in a magnetic way. Your desires, whether conscious or not, have brought you to this point. The other side is not a faraway place. It is here with you all the time, existing on a different physical plane or in a different dimension than that of your own. Your experience doesn't have to include a "journey" in which you feel as though you have left your body and are traveling to another location. The contact and connection can happen in your own body or mind. You may not visualize anything. You may only have a physical sense of calm. You may experience different temperature changes or tingling. All of these experiences are valid. This is why it is important to give yourself the time and space to experience without interruption.

Lokar: What is going on with you at other times may also be significant, indicating that energetic channels are being put in place. During the quiet time you may experience changes in body temperature. If you get cold when going into your session then place a blanket in your lap or on the back of the chair so you can easily place it around you and continue relatively undisturbed. If this chill occurs regularly wrap up as you start. On the other side of the coin it is just as likely you will get hot. Your temperature may rise very quickly as if you were having a sudden burst of fever. These may occur at any time as the energetic adjustments are being caused by a being which has very little sense of time. Your guide acts when conditions and opportunities present themselves for the most efficient upgrades in channeling energy.

Some will experience a slight, but temporary, euphoria as well as moments of joy. A feeling of gentle love of life is also a common experience when this work is in progress. Miriam and Jerry have both had these experiences in their process of increased awareness. These indicators that work is being done from the other levels don't always take place while you are in a session. Jerry and Miriam have also experienced these phenomena while reading, watching television, sitting in a waiting room or just doing some casual activity. At some point the thought will pop into your head that the work to open a clear channel is being done.

It is easy to get to the other side, because it is no farther away than the heads are away from tails on the flip side of a coin. The two are joined one must have the other for the coin to be complete. We often make things hard on ourselves. Be patient and trust in the legion of helpers who wish to greet you and help you through your earthly experience.

Chapter 4: Should I let anyone in and how will I know who?

Lokar: Beings, when they pass from the earthly plane through the process you call death, make choices. Those who choose to go into the light have their vibrational energy changed and begin the process of adjusting to their new spiritual existence.

As the reader, be very clear on this point: you have your own religious beliefs which in no way are contrary to what goes on in channeling. Your beliefs may include Heaven, Hell and the Devil. Other beliefs may include reincarnation and the related religious teachings which embrace that concept. None of this is contrary to the channeling. The bottom line is that if you believe in any form of afterlife you can channel without any fear of being contradictory to your belief system.

The title of this chapter implies that you need to be selective with whom you set up communication. Be very clear that your conversations with other side entities are a matter of choice. You are not expected to talk with everyone on the earthly plane and you make choices all the time as to who and what you talk about. This chapter will give you methods and insights as to how you can control the communication while channeling using illustrations relative to other belief systems so the concepts and procedures will coalesce.

The formats of the afterlife which have been embellished and invented by humans are personal teachings. These inspirations handed down through various religions differ greatly. They are the same, in general, as they describe a place of goodness, righteous being and great joy. The beings in these places are the ones you wish to contact. These other dimensional entities you may call angels, masters, avatars, spirit guides, and more.

In most teachings there are the other places, hells of various types ranging from spiritual holding places where afterlife arrivals work out their earthly existence, to places of total condemnation. The bottom line is there are differing levels in the afterlife and they contain entities which range from confused, and not wholesome, to mischievous and evil at the lower levels. Many of these entities are not condemned to eternal bondage at these levels. They can help themselves out of their situation.

Be cautioned and aware this is not a place for earthly missionaries.

We often hear of individuals who have had a near death experience and claim to have moved into and through a tunnel of light to a glorious existence with all sorts of wonders only to be pulled back into their body and this life. This gateway of light is a path to the afterlife which we all deserve but, as with all things, there is a choice. Some choose not to take this path and they cling to a past which to others would seem trivial. These wandering souls thrill on physical events which they had in their earthly life. They have locked themselves into a mundane existence. This lower level existence is referred to as a purgatory or Limbo by some, or the second physical by others. It mimics an earthly existence but is a sham. The citizens of this place have chosen to stay in the fantasy of their previous existence and not progress into the light.

When you open up a channel for communication you do so in the light. The beings from above have set up energies which form a protective cocoon around the channeler into which they can put their energetic vibrations, appearing to the channeler as forms of communication. As the channeler writes, speaks or thinks a question or other communication this energetic envelope transmits over the gap of a few inches to the receiving entity. Beings of the afterlife are in another dimension and the vibrational cocoon which is created allows an exchange to occur. This is so loving of our individual guides and represents a great effort on their part. They are our devoted companions. Once asked, your guides and angels will maintain this opening to the other side. The channeler's task is to keep their self in a state of grace while communicating.

Occasionally an entity will try to communicate that is not your chosen guide. Someone from another realm tries to but in. It may be an important message from another person's guide or it may be an undesirable. You must be wary of these communications. The key to the contact is always asking each individual whether they are from the light and their name. Once that is done ask them to state their business or the reason for the contact.

If the entity does not respond to the initial question of name and light origin instruct them to be gone and tell them they have no business with you. On rare occasion they may persist. Ask your guide to remove them and be done with it. Thank your guide and ask if it is appropriate to continue the session or close it.

These occurrences are rare and can happen if the channeler is under the influence of a medical substance which makes them woozy. Don't drink and drive and don't channel under the influence; you may get more than you bargained for.

Your channeling experience will be full of many meaningful moments which will enhance your life. As always there is only one person responsible for your happiness, and that is you. The choices you make as a result of the information you receive from channeling are yours exclusively. You live your life as you see fit and follow another's advice or consul as you choose.

El-Israel: The question of entry, that is the entry of a separate entity into one's energy body, must be addressed. At this point in the spiritual and energetic evolution of the average human, we are not advocating allowing beings, of any kind, into one's energy body. In other words, don't be a host for another entity at this stage of your channeling. Your task is to become comfortable with, and aware of, the way your higher self and guides communicate with you.

The purpose is to establish a connection that allows for your spiritual growth and a feeling of comfort.

As you go through your time on this planet and in your life, you have come to realize that the life you have chosen to live on this plane is one in which difficulty is intended to bring you accelerated growth. You are an evolved spirit who has chosen to make great strides in your development by subjecting yourself to much pain and suffering at this time and on this plane. Because the energy of your dimension is shifting, the need for this suffering is coming to a close and you will be able to grow spiritually without the anguish and angst of previous times.

Leal: It does not matter what your position is in society in this life. You all are here in service to a higher calling and the ultimate goal is the realization that all of mankind must work together to establish peace and harmony. In this way we are able to experience a daily "Heaven on Earth". You are able to experience joy and compassion in even the most menial tasks because you are in communication with a higher source which reveals to you that you are meeting your goals and achieving growth in a loving and fluid manner that does not require stress and distress.

After you have become familiar with the sensual experience of connection with yourself and your guides, and you feel completely comfortable in the safety of your channeling and your ability to determine whether the beings making contact with you are there for your highest good and of the light, then you may seek out further spiritual advice on whether or not to host. In our opinion, this activity is not yet safe for most humans and should be avoided. Your safety and comfort are of primary concern and your enlightenment to the constant experience of living in communion with God and the light beings working for you development is the goal.

El-Israel: Consequently, you should not be letting any being "in". The act of establishing communication and allowing beings to enter your protected energy space should feel as though you are being approached, not taken over. Beings that make an effort to take over one's body and use it for their advantage are not beings from the light. If you ever feel as though this is happening or experience any discomfort, immediately ask your guides to clear the energy and reestablish a protective bubble around you. Specifically ask, out loud or in your mind, for angels to usher out any being that has entered your space without loving intent toward you. When you feel as though the space has been cleared, you should reconnect first with your higher self.

Lokar: There is a model which may be helpful to put the afterlife and our present life into order. This arrangement can give the reader a sense of the categories of the beings which may be contacted while channeling.

In our present life we all have a higher self, some may refer to it as a level of the subconscious, a super conscience, or an aspect of our soul, any personal designation can serve the purpose. We will refer to it as the higher self. This higher self resides within us it is our inner connection with our mission in life. Unfortunately it seems very distant to most humans and seldom if ever directly communicated with. This higher self is you, as close to perfect as you can be; it will guide you to fulfill your earthly mission and can be easily contacted through the basic techniques of channeling described in this book. When communicating with the higher self the response to questions will be directed to the best way to complete your mission at that particular moment. Again be reminded it is you in the conscious life who decides which path to take. A well-established contact with your higher self will reveal your life mission, if appropriate.

The regions of the afterlife are no farther than a few inches away, invisible because they are of another dimension. These dimensions are infinite and boggle the mind. For their nature is so alien to us that when we try to picture them the beings therein often appear as images of men and women. These beings appear more closely as pillars of light. To you the different beings of the afterlife would appear the same until their particular vibrational energy differences can be discerned by the channel.

The order presented here is not indicative of importance, but does give a general idea of what the various entities' jobs are in the other dimensions.

Higher Self

Communication with the higher self is the clearest inner communication an individual can have. The higher self has a lot of names. One might refer to it as the soul, while another perceives of it as a super conscience, or divine self; it is the essence of your being in this lifetime. This essence has one grand purpose fulfillment. To this end we often engage our higher self as a still small voice.

Initially you begin the communication cycle with a request. The higher self is more easily contacted through prayer or a beginning meditation in which you remain aware. The communication will take various forms as individuals perceive the connection in different ways. Some will receive messages which are vocal while others will get mind pictures or feelings. These communications will come to you in the most receptive way possible. The process is a spiritual experience.

The nature of the communication will be about your mission. Everyone's mission is the same. We are all going Home. We all understand ourselves as being the essence of God. We are Divine and our higher self won't let us forget it. It is necessary for most of us to get a better sense of what we are to do in this lifetime to fulfill our mission of self-understanding. The whole nature of being Divine makes demands on us as we conduct ourselves in this lifetime. All religions have rules of conduct which give us an outward set of rules to follow. Your inner self has more refined rules of conduct which will lead you to a more enriched life. The talents which you possess in this lifetime along with your inner passions serve yourself and mankind; these are outward manifestations of the higher self guiding you in recognizing your purpose and leading you to realize the joy of living.

The quick self-talk which comes from the higher self in the form of immediate advice is identifiable as different from spirit guide advice. At first there may be confusion as to which is which. This is understandable until you become aware of the subtle difference between the outer energy and self-communication.

Archangels

Archangels are those who see to the governing of planets and local portions of the planetary energy. They are grand scale thinkers and have never been human.

Angels

Angels do communicate with, guide, guard and protect humans. The guardian angel depicted on drawings is a stylized version of how they often surround a young one who has wandered unaware into some danger. Many adults have been visited by angels who appear for the moment in human form to render aide. This is one of the jobs which they have. Oskar who has taken on the task of enhancing the energy levels of Jerry and is acting as general counsel in the writing of this book also takes on duties for running the planet earth. Many angels are involved in the operation of what physicists would describe as the laws of physics. They supervise and see to the harmony of the universe without interfering with the natural evolvement of mankind's choice. They work in groups under the guidance of Archangels.

A special group of angels is the Heavenly Choir which expresses joy through the wonderful songs it weaves. Many earthlings have sat quietly and heard the melodic tones of their voices in their mind's ear.

Avatars

Avatars are high minded individuals who have taken on the task of guiding the physical beings of a planet. They may choose to work with the ecology of a forest and have a group of spirit guides which maintain the flora, fauna and function of nature on that part of the planet. What has been observed as animal instinct is often the result of a spirit guide directing a species through a specific thought process.

These beings have all been human at one time and have risen to their position through hard work and dedication to the task. There is much work being done to keep the planetary ecology on the right track. There is much remorse and consternation about how certain groups of the human race treat the planet. These dedicated beings yearn for the harmony of man and the planet. They guide humans in an effort to hold the planet together. They lay out programs for other guides to relate to those who are listening. This is one reason this book is being written. More humans on the planet need to be listening to what the guides have to offer us to make harmonious choices in running our lives and the planet. At this moment in time too few are active; because they don't know what to do they are overwhelmed. The chaos of the planet is increasing and only through the efforts of individuals attuned to a better thought will reverse this destructive trend.

Spirit guides

Spirit guides work with individuals. They will often take on a specific task and then relinquish their position to another who has greater expertise. Be aware none of us are 'all knowing', we are not God, nor are we God's. We give you the information of many lives of experience so that you may decide as to what is best for you to do. Spirits guides are a fantastic resource and will help any who ask. We have chosen to help you and those around you through communication of ideas which are intended to open avenues of a variety of actions.

The beings in the afterlife which have crossed over recently are not usually available for this type of guidance until they have gone through their personal life's review. All such contacts must be done through your individual guide and will usually come in the form of a related message. Attempts at direct communication with the recently departed will often lead to uninvited entities which will say anything for the thrill of having someone to play with. Always ask if from the light and the name and purpose.

Those of us which I have described have one grand purpose: to express God's design in us all through serving one another.

Leal: It is with great joy that we have come to an era where those of you who are reading this are capable of opening up to the higher vibrations of light and are able to make connections. All of the beings Lokar has defined are here for your protection and are functioning out of love and a desire to maintain and be instrumental in the evolution of humankind to a cohesive and loving place of oneness with all that is. Our goal is give you the strength of conviction to live your life's purpose and be happy in all you do, knowing that whatever task you do is one of great purpose in the course of the spiritual evolution of the planet. It is with great love and pleasure that we are here for you, to answer your questions and provide you with the comfort that comes with knowledge. All light beings are blessed to be in your service as you struggle to find joy and raise the frequency of your beautiful planet to a level that will support the next stage of spiritual development and a second coming.

Remember that guides are available to answer your questions and give you insight into possible repercussions of any decisions you make. They are not here to give you all the answers and for you to follow without judgment on your part. Communication with your higher self will give you perspective as to the role you are currently playing in the energetic evolution of the planet and mankind. This should give you some peace at whatever level and in whatever capacity you are living to fulfill your role. If your job, currently, is to provide care for the new evolution of spiritually attuned children entering at this time, you will be able to find joy in that convocation. Likewise, if you are given large amounts of money and instructed to provide for others philanthropically, you will find joy in this, as well. This concept is related to the idea of Dharma held in eastern belief, but refined. The goal is for those whose responsibilities are well compensated to provide for those whose role is great, but whose financial compensation is less. However, in all instances and situations, you are provided with the free will to choose your actions. Our hope is that, with guidance, you will follow your heart and choose to live in community with your higher self and in alignment with your higher purpose for the benefit of all mankind.

Chapter 5: What will I experience?

Lokar: When an individual first attempts to channel they are never sure of what is going on. The voices in their head are their own so they think they are having an imaginary flight. You might have trouble getting comfortable in the seat you're in. A whole series of thoughts, body twitches and outside interruptions flood in as you try to become quiet. This is all very distracting in the beginning when you are trying so hard to find out if you can do it.

After you have prepared yourself with pad and paper or a recording device, relax. For those of you who pray regularly or use meditation, this quieting process will not be a problem. Others may have to use a relaxing exercise to achieve a state of quiet. Once you have reached a state of relative calm, the initial question is a request to contact your spirit guide. By reading this book and showing an initial interest, work from the other plane has already been in progress to establish a set of guides to work with you. For this reason, you will often get a quick response. If you use a pad and pen, write both sides of the conversation, this method is the usual beginning technique. Writing the question often solidifies the thought of the petitioner. Then wait and write whatever comes into mind. If you get a thought like, 'this is stupid' write it down. You might get a very quick answer as to why it's not. The whole process at first is full of doubt and sometimes a little frustration because what seems to be coming through is a mixture of self thoughts and other thoughts. Don't expect dramatic results in the first few sessions. The amount of energetic adjustment is tremendous and requires a great effort from your guides.

In this state of relaxation you should not drift off into a meditative state, remain conscious so you can record your experience. As you learn to hold a conscious rapport with your guide you will be able to do this at any time during your waking hours. Jerry often holds conversations with himself and his guide while doing mundane tasks. This self talk is best kept silent or at least under the guise of using a cell phone if you are in a public place.

In every session check the source of the information you receive and whether they are of the light. After a while you begin to feel the energy of your guide and can tell the difference between them and another entity. When you hit this point of confidence in your communication it is still wise to ask the above questions at any time you feel something is different. Your guide will never be offended.

Let us address the beginning mind chatter and its value to the process of establishing a viable and useful contact. As you record what seems to be nonsense bits and pieces of genuine thought are stimulating the various parts of your brain to become more receptive. The vibrational quality of the words and there combination is an easier way of energizing areas in the brain so that you become more receptive. These word combinations are often interspersed with your individual thoughts. These may seem to be interruptions in the process, but are responses to the adjustments. To many it comes as a relief when actual conversation starts being exchanged. Now you usually get a charge of excitement at this moment and are concerned that you might break contact. Calm down and get right into the next questions.

Some of you may make a preliminary list of questions to ask just to start the ball rolling. You might ask why is channeling important for me? What do I need to do to make the communication clearer? How can you help me with a specific issue? Your personal belief system will be honored by your guides as they tailor the answers to fit your perception of life.

It is important to note that spirit guides and those in the upper level will not define or identify your mission in life. Your higher self will do that and we will discuss that process later. The guides will however help you with the process of achieving your mission as you move on through the challenges in your earthly life. This is a step by step endeavor and will take some earthly time.

It is important to remember guides are simply advisors and sources of information to help you through your activities and issues. You must always make your own decisions and judgments on a particular issue. Your guides will cut off the connection if you start doing everything they tell you. Their purpose is to help not to make all your decisions for you. You alone steer the course of your life.

El-Isreal: There are many ways in which one experiences the connection with a higher being, including one's higher self. You are limited by the genetic makeup of your physical body to methods that are consistent with your physical vibration on this planet. Just as people are able to learn in different ways, communication with the other side comes to individuals in ways that work best for that person. It is common to see a light surrounding you and feel a presence of energy that surrounds and enfolds. For some, their attention is drawn to what is commonly known as the "third eye" or area between and slightly above the eyes and bridge of the nose. Think of it as looking cross-eyed and up slightly with your eyes closed. You may feel a pressure or vibration in this area or you may simply notice that your attention is drawn to this location. These are normal experiences.

For those who are more visual, you will probably "see" a golden light that descends to enter at the third eye or may surround you. It is common to sense light beings that follow this same path directly to the third eye from in front and above you. Non-light entities or earthbound entities will try to approach you from the right or left sides. These are not the beings you wish to be in communication with at this time. If this happens, please ask them to leave and re-establish a protective circle of light around you and verbalize your intent to work only with your higher self or light beings that are present for your highest good.

Light beings may appear to you in a hazy type of physical form. They will be figures of light but may not have much definition. Some people will see faces or parts of faces, such as eyes or smiling mouths. Do not be concerned if you do not see a whole being or something that looks like a person. It is very difficult for us to maintain a form consistent with your perception of what people look like. We are able to take many forms in our plane and change as is necessary to our task so how we look is more fluid than your physical appearance. We try to come in a form that appeals to you, however.

For those who have visual communication, you may find it easiest to establish meanings for visual stimuli. For instance, you may ask that a yes response appear as a head nodding up and down and a no response as a back and forth. When your ability is strengthened, you may ask to see visual outcomes of taking certain actions or a picture of what you should be doing in your life at the moment. Pay attention to how the pictures make you feel when you see them and go with your gut feeling or instinct when forming your decisions about how to proceed.

Leal: Others may sense our presence as a vibration or pressure. You may feel tingling in your extremities or a pressure at the location of the third eye. You may feel a change in temperature or a cool or warm breeze that engulfs you. It is not uncommon for people to simply have a sense of the communication or answers to their questions. If you are an individual that senses our presence through vibration, you may ask for and establish a method of communication. For instance, you may ask that you receive answers to questions in a "yes/no" format where you sense a slight increase in pressure for a yes and a decrease for a no. Your guides are happy to use whatever method works for you to be able to strengthen your ability to correctly receive responses to your questions.

Others may sense the presence of a guide aurally. You may hear a sound that pleases you. The noise will seem to begin at the back of the head and move around to the ears. It will enter and resonate in the head. This sound will be comforting and peaceful. You may hear voices that will guide you. Please be sure to ask if the nature the being who speaks to you and whether or not that being comes from the light. For people who are able to hear, you may begin with yes/ no questions as your ability to hear answers is refined. Later on, you may be able to have full conversations in which the answers to your requests are explained in a depth by which you are able to weigh pros and cons of different actions and possible outcomes.

Let us take a moment to introduce a new high master guide, Seth, who has waited until this time to make his presence know because of the necessary matching of energy frequencies between himself and the scribe Jerry.

Seth: There comes a time in the channeling experience when the individuals' energy levels change. It is a natural consequence of the process of being connected to the other side. New vistas open in terms of experiencing the communication more clearly. The process flows more clearly, but also becomes enhanced. Through channeling you add another dimension to your being. This dimension will become second nature if you employ it regularly and will serve you in ways which you cannot imagine in the beginning. Your attitude toward life will change into one of calm and harmony. Those things which others find stressful and major problems in their lives will not affect your life in the same way for you will know what needs to be done or more importantly that nothing needs doing. There is a great satisfaction in letting things evolve with their own process and nature without interference. Life flows for you harmoniously when you are connected with authority to your supportive friends of the other side. Problems will still arise, but solutions will be readily available, often more than one choice will be presented so you can decide your path. It is our great honor and joy to be able to serve for once the door between dimensions is asked to be opened we here will work diligently to fulfill our purpose, to guide.

Lokar: Once a suitable contact is established you will often find that the initial contact guide will remove themselves from the conversation and another guide will step in. this is particularly true if you are working on an ongoing task. In these situations an expert in the field will step up to give you assistance and guide you through a process. No guide is all knowing and when a project involves a great deal of effort we guides often work as a group to give the best result possible. This is why it is so important that as guides we have had human experiences on this planet. Our advice is an opinion as to how you might proceed in regard to the issue at hand. We may have a great deal of expertise, but we are not perfect.

If, for whatever reason, the advice you receive from a guide doesn't make sense or doesn't feel right ask for clarification. Often a simple, "Why?" question helps you get to the underlying point and the advice becomes clear. Always the choice remains with you. Have fun! Share your concerns, your triumphs and even a good laugh with your new found friends.

As you become more in tune with your guides you will feel the individual's energy differently for each personality. This is proper in that each spirit brings different gifts, solutions and advice to a situation. One might think that a great cosmic argument ensues as to who gets to communicate with the person that is channeling. This is human thinking and very far from what actually goes on. Each guide recognizes what the other brings to the question at hand in the form of advice. There is a gentle interaction between the guides as they perceive which message carries the most importance at the moment. Often one guide will act as a spokesperson for another so a connection doesn't have to be reestablished to communicate.

All we do in this process of communication is try to make your life more fruitful and abundant, hopefully to shorten your journey to understanding who you really are.

Leal: It is important to remember that you are able to determine what feels comfortable for you. You should not feel pressured or invaded. At all times an experience of calm and love is normal and desired. If you find yourself in a place of discomfort physically, mentally or emotionally, stop and ask your guide to recalibrate to a frequency that is comfortable for you. In many cases, we believe we have achieved a perfect connection but you may experience some "static". By letting your guide know and asking to be better attuned, a recalibration can occur to ensure that your experience is enjoyable. After all, we want to keep you coming back! When Miriam first began to channel, she felt vibrationally discomforted. She expressed this and we were able to adjust our frequency to be more resonant with that of her own.

El-Israel: Your experience in channeling is personal to you. For this reason, it does no good to compare yours to anyone else's. The point is to become more and more aware of subtle changes in your own energy field that let you know that communication has been established along with the ability to receive messages and suggestions. As you become aware, you will be able to focus in at any time and receive immediate responses. In an instant from the time you determine you will open to your guides, you will feel the subtle energy shift. Eventually, you will be able to receive feedback in any situation and, in this way, live in constant communion with your higher self and your guides, understanding and living in the joy of God's will for you and experiencing your connection to all.

Miriam: I feel as though it is important to include some personal experience here for the reader. When I first began, my intention was not to be a channel. I was in the habit of meditating, achieving a state of calm. Part of my meditation included establishing an area of protection and white light around me. Having read Sylvia Browne's suggestions and meditations on how to connect with my spirit guide I was able, first, to receive visual pictures in my mind's eye of people, places or activities. Sometimes I would ask yes/no questions and see a head nodding in response. Later, I began to use the same form of visual communication to ask questions for others of their guides.

One day, in an effort to communicate with my mother's guide, a beautiful golden light came to me from above and surrounded me. I felt as though my body was humming and I saw the outline of a very large light being. Without thinking, I began to write his letter to her.

After my exposure to Sanaya Roman's books on channeling, I determined I would establish communication with and open up to speaking for, my highest guide. Settling into a meditative state of calm relaxation and establishing a protective circle of light came first. I asked to meet her. The vibration around me changed significantly and I began to feel discomfort with the humming sensation in the energy field surrounding and in my body. I told her that I was not comfortable and asked that she be aided to adjust the frequency to a more comfortable level. In a matter of seconds, the uncomfortable vibration ceased and I was in full communication with my guide, Daphnae. Now, I can be walking in the park or sitting at my desk, turn my focus in to ask a question, and she comes to me. I have several guides who work with me as needed: Jofar gives me insight into daily matters and provides me with lists, Samuel instructs me in matters of health and physical well-being, and Daphnae, for whom I speak, answers my questions about spirituality and provides answers to others through my intuitive readings. El-Israel and Leal come to me solely for the purposes of writing this book. All of these have a different energy "personality" and feel different.

Jerry: I will also take a moment at this time to help the reader understand how the process varies when you first discover or ask to channel. I was on a vacation trip with my wife when we stopped for a little sightseeing and shopping in Trinidad, CO. I found myself drawn to a particular shop off the main street and while my wife shopped I picked up a book called *Angelspeake*, by Trudy Griswold, about getting in touch with one's angels. Previous to this point I have had a checkered experience with healing, meditation and various other philosophical pursuits. While on vacation I had the opportunity to follow the instructions therein and eventually get a solid connection with an angel called Oskar. This connection was a daily affair asking for bits of advice and was experimental fun.

When I transferred from a note pad to a word processor, things really got interesting. I call myself a computer dinosaur because I typed using three fingers, not always the same ones, yet here I was being instructed to get in front of the keyboard. From some distant typing class I remembered where to put my fingers of stone. Within a matter of days I was typing fluently and receiving messages from several guides. Lokar, who dictates portions of this book, announced that I was to write a book. Within 24 hours, Miriam wrote to me that her guides said we were to collaborate on a book. My energy levels have been augmented no less than 4 times in the span of 3 months and I can clearly tell when a new arrival wishes to speak. I hear the words they say conversationally and type them as they are said. This experience has been a wonder to say the least.

El-Israel: It is important to understand that Miriam and Jerry have some similarity in their reception of the incoming frequencies of communication. They are both auto-writers. This is not the only way to establish communication with the guides. What the reader should take away from their information is that they were able to identify various different beings, sensing a shift in the vibrational energy as new guides come in. As Miriam stated, each of us has our own frequency "personality", as do each of you. Over time both she and Jerry have established communication with a number of beings. Their role is to write a book that will be helpful in the evolution of mankind. Your role may be different and you may interact with only one, or many more, beings. Let your experience be your own and you will find you become more and more aware of subtle energy shifts and the transmission will become clearer.

Seth: As with all things you must exercise patience. The process you are experiencing used to take people years to cultivate. At the present time you are given a great opportunity as years have become weeks and even days. The main deterrent to your progress is your own impatience, don't give up on the connection to quickly or expect too much from the beginning information which you receive. These beginnings are full of adjustments and corrections to refine the vibrations which facilitate the connection. All connections have to be refined, modified and enhanced this takes time. We are in the process of making available a technology of spirit to the coming age, one which is necessary for the preservation and growth of mankind on this planet. Without a sufficient number of the present inhabitants of earth bringing forth the energies and communications from the higher dimensions the present civilization could find itself doomed to collapse. The guides urge you to accept the responsibility of your own evolutionary progress and set the tone for a truly glorious age.

Chapter 6: How should my channeling session be closed?

Leal: The experience of channeling is one which, if done correctly and in the protective light, leaves one feeling calm and happy. You will experience a true sense of satisfaction and a joy at knowing you are no longer alone in your efforts in life. The goal is to carry these feelings with you at every moment of every day. However, this may take some practice and you must not allow yourself to be in a vulnerable position. It is appropriate to ask that your angels or even an archangel, live with you and be present in your home and in all tasks to provide you with protection.

As your vibrational energies change, you will become more of a light being in your own dimension, radiating love and life to others. As you can imagine, this radiation of love will attract others to you to cull energy and happiness from your own. There are those who would like, even subconsciously, to drain you and take your positive energy for themselves. You must find a balance between giving and receiving.

El-Israel: There is a common misconception that you do not have control over other people using your energy. Body workers often experience this. They feel drained after a few sessions and believe some of their own personal energy has gone into the healing of others. This can only happen if you allow it to be so. However, you can also be a conduit that catalyzes an energy shift in others without depleting your own. All lower frequencies can be made to vibrate at a higher level, in resonance with higher level frequencies to which they are exposed, through resonance. The goal, as you interact with others is to connect with them in a fashion that will allow their frequency to begin to resonate with yours. This will be explained in further detail in the subsequent chapter. First you must be able to close your session in a way that allows you to maintain the energy shifts you have experienced in a protective manner.

We often think to prepare a space energetically with light and set up a form of protection against negative energies and evil. However, at the end of the session, in a state of happiness and contentment, it is easy to walk away from the space, leaving ourselves open to the influx of vibrational shifts of the environment outside the circle or those of other people. In order to maintain the progress made through the channeling and the recalibration of your frequency to one more resonant with that of a higher being, you must shield yourself from the unwitting draining by others and the attraction of negative. Negative energies are drawn to the light because it can transmute them, little by little, allowing them to be elevated to higher level without work. If you give a person dinner, they will eat. If you buy them food and show them how to make dinner, they will be much better off in the long run. Likewise, if you give negative energies an opportunity to be transmuted they will accept and begin to be elevated toward the light. If they must work toward their progression themselves, they will be able to learn and grow more in the future and the goal will still be achieved.

Seth: You are essentially a light as the bible says, "a light under a bushel." When you come out of a session your bushel has been lifted and a little more light is visible to others. You are becoming a beacon of goodness capable of many new things as you progress, to the wonderment of others. How attractive you become is, to a degree, how much light you emit. Others of all sorts are attracted to you because they seek the light themselves and basking in yours is easier than doing the work themselves.

Jesus' admonition to work out your own salvation involves, in part, increasing your vibrational energy to become more attuned to your own light, the light being which you are. This process is natural to the elevation of your understanding of being. You must know that you are working out your own salvation and so are those who would ride on your efforts and not their own. When you affirm that each person must develop on their own path, they are severed from you. This brings them to a basic realization about themselves and they must respond by looking inward to their own process for salvation. In most cases this is an unconscious occurrence and the shift in the individual is subtle. When you close you must know this and affirm this about all you meet and have transactions with. It becomes a mantra to confirm that others are responsible for themselves. Jesus gave many hints as to how we may help our fellow travelers in realizing the true nature of their being, but he also admonished that they must do it themselves.

Therefore, upon closing your session, be aware of the increase of your personal attraction to others. Declare that you and all mankind seek the light of their own being, the light which is the source and animates them with the life force and makes them who they are. You become a beacon, a lighthouse shining forth in an ever increasing splendor; guiding others but keeping aloof from their attempts to get your energy through means which are not their own accomplishment. Imagining yourself as this beacon on the top of a tower you make it very difficult for others to reach the source of your vibrational energy, you can share your light energy but not its core source. The light from the lighthouse guides but is intended to do so only from within.

El-Isreal: Those who have experience with meditation will know that many end in the same fashion. One is usually instructed to come back to one's body or the present moment and, when ready, open their eyes. This is not exactly what is happening. Those people who experience interaction with their guides visually, or who are using creative visualization to manifest in their lives, feel as though they have travelled to a different location and must return and re-enter their own body. While some are experienced in advanced meditative techniques and may project astrally, one is always connected to, and residing in, the body on this plane. What you experience is a subtle shift to another dimensional reality in which you are able to perceive different energetic beings and see the world from a different perspective. Using your imagination takes you to a place in which new realities are created dimensionally. A return to your body is really only a refocusing of your senses back to the dimensions in which you are functioning vibrationally in your human state.

The first step of closing a session is to consciously return your focus to the present and re-establish your presence in the earthly dimension. This may feel as though you are returning to your body, or more specifically, like your focus is coming back into your head. You may feel a heaviness as your new vibrational pattern realigns itself and adjusts to functioning in the earthly dimension. You may feel a warming sensation as you reconnect with the physical body and its warmth. You may experience a slight popping in the ears or pressure. All of these experiences are normal and serve to let you know that you are closing your senses and vibration to input from unwanted sources, much as a child who covers his ears to avoid instructions from parents. You are making the choice to only accept input from the sources you choose.

Leal: The next step is one that many people either do not know or do not understand to be important. You must establish two things: that you are not giving away your energy to others and that the light you project serves as an example to, but not a fix-all for, others whose current state would benefit from your shift in energy. In order for these to happen, you must establish a protective barrier between yourself and other people. They should be able to sense the new lighter being in you but not have access to it without your permission. There are several ways to establish this. You may ask that your guide send you light energy that surrounds you and closes you off from others. In some ways this is the easiest method as you are not doing the protective work for yourself and may be a good starting point for those who are new to this form of communication. As time progresses, and your experience and awareness of the new vibrational energies expand, it will become your responsibility to create this type of barrier for yourself. After all, there are still lessons to be learned and you must take responsibility for your own learning and growth.

As you become more familiar with visualizing, feeling, vocalizing or hearing on a different level, you will use the method that works best for you. Some may say out loud, at the end of their session, "I now close my session and establish that these energetic gains are secure in my energetic body. I am protected." You may visualize a soothing pink light surrounding you and a cocoon of two-sided mirrors that will reflect any negativity away and positive energy back to you. Some will feel a blanket of protection that wraps around them and prevents access. Any method is appropriate as long as you sense a shift in your energy field that makes you feel secure and safe.

Lokar: For some the session never ends. The formal closing does occur taking one from the serene state of contact back into the everyday events of the human world. The protective mantel you create through asking and the inspiration of your higher self is a shield which will provide you with protection from intrusion of both worlds. However you can maintain a conscious contact with your guide throughout your daily activities. It is well to have a sense of what your purpose is when you finally sustain an ongoing contact. This personal purpose is not necessarily some grand goal or question; instead you may just seek to have guidance in making more informed decisions on how to conduct your life. We who guide are not put off by what others might consider mundane or every day questions and problems. As more of you use us as a resource you will find that you have a friend with you at all times to consult with, converse with and help you with the day's rigors. A businessman may want to consider if the time of an appointment is opportune, a housewife may be in question about the evenings menu, while a young lady may question if she should accept a date which has been offered. These are common occurrences and have meaning in the everyday flow of human life. When you learn to be connected, whenever you need advice you will find the channeling process a great resource. Being thus connected throughout your days the session in one sense never closes.

Leal: The last step in your closing practice should be one of confirmation. Much as some religious bodies believe that once you are confirmed you have brought the spirit of Jesus to live within you, you are confirming God's presence. The act of confirmation brings you in to the whole, connecting you with all that is, energetically. It is a reminder that you are part of the tribe and a member of a greater community that functions in peace and under the influence of a higher power. It does not matter what your belief system includes in terms of the origin of that higher power. Each time you reaffirm your confirmation you strengthen your connection to the divine and the ties that bind a planetary community in the goal of bringing peace to all humankind. Through your guides, you are able to maintain a constant line of communication between your physical self, your higher self and the guides who have been sent to reveal your life's purpose to you and help you through your process of giving, receiving and learning. It is important to recognize the connection has been made and to give thanks for the understanding that has developed in you.

It is always good to express appreciation and gratitude. We give gifts to others as a physical expression of our appreciation for the roles they play in our lives. In the past, humans gave sacrifices to God and their spiritual guides in much the same way. Spiritually, humankind has evolved to a place where such physical shows of appreciation are not warranted. However, now that communication between you and your guides has been established, it is appropriate to thank them for the work they are doing for you and the growth you are experiencing as a result. This can be done verbally by simply saying, "Thank you", or in your mind. You may send love to the guides from your heart or bow with hands placed in front of the heart. Any expression is welcomed and allows for your connections to strengthen. The act of giving thanks strengthens your bond and draws you closer to your Divine source. Always close by expressing gratitude to your

guides and to God for your awareness of the
support that is offered to you.

Chapter 7: Now that I channel, what responsibility do I have?

Seth: The responsibility of channeling is to use the information to enhance your life and the lives of the community in which you live. There are many opportunities to use the information to help those around you, your family and friends, but what of the others you come in contact with? This is where the greater dynamic of channeling is exposed. You are now closer to your true state, your vibration affects all who are in you vicinity, you are a beacon and a magnet all rolled into one. As your light intensity grows people will respond to your elevated vibrations, being drawn directly to you or paying particular attention to your actions. This may seem to make your life more public as what you say and do draws more attention from those you come in contact with, and in a sense this exposure may cause you some concern in the beginning. Those of you that have a nature to be more of a recluse and be in the background when confronted with a group will find the new attention which you draw possibly uncomfortable. Children, animals, strangers and even those with whom you have had little contact will suddenly become talkative and even helpful joining you in your regular activities.

All this may be well and good, don't get on a soap box and start preaching, be very careful not to make the human mistake of trying to sell the product which you have just discovered. Instead follow your heart and the advice which will become your ever present companion. Your guides will fill you with the information to act in the appropriate way when you interact with the people in your surroundings. You are a living example of what the channeling process can do in a person's life. Your example is what will attract others to you and have them seek the secret of your calm demeanor and the ease with which you flow through your daily activities. You are being yourself when you do this and as yourself the love of living flows out through you attracting others and causing them to inquire as to your secret of life.

Oskar: The heavens rejoice and the angels sing with the dawning of each new awareness of the nature of being. When you share this new awareness through your actions with others serving yourself and mankind, you are one with your Creator an enlightened being, a being of light. Bless you, bless you, and bless you all.

Lokar: You must always be yourself this is your greatest responsibility. You will receive a lot of information and as you practice the channeling and you become a walking channel through which your guides can funnel information about the daily activities. You will have to filter out what you choose to do. No one makes those decisions for you. You act and chose not to act on the information or the advice given. You must be very clear about this for this is crucial to you progressing and not collapsing. Those who have channeled in the past and have collapsed themselves into the information they were getting soon found the fountain slow to a trickle and then be shut off. Your guides guide they do not live your life for you. When these poor individuals struggled to reach for their guides and found nothing they often sought solace from other entities, a few fortunately got in contact with their higher self and got straightened around to being responsible for themselves, others started taking bad advice which at first sounded good and ended up in all sorts of mental and personal dilemmas. Keep your own counsel always. If something doesn't sound right check out the source. Stop and ask the two pertinent questions of who you are in contact with, and if they are from the light. Don't get complacent and not ask when there is any doubt or if the information seems strange. Then you can ask about the consequences and possible results of following this advice. After you have gotten all the information from one source check with another guide or angel, you get a second or even a third opinion. After you have finished your process of information gathering follow your own best counsel. No one in this system is perfect, when we get there we are home and all of this no longer matters, but in the meantime an eternity awaits for some while others will shorten their paths considerably and no longer have the necessity of an earthly body to come back to.

The responsibilities of channeling are many; they hinge on propriety. When we are proper we remain true to ourselves, treat others with kindness and go about our business with joy. I cannot over emphasize the importance of being you as your vibration increases to a higher sense of being. Others will see changes in you; your actions will change in various ways often to cause loved ones some concern. You may be questioned as to your health or your mental state. You may start to enjoy an aspect of life which previously was not important. This all is harmless when viewed in the big picture of a life, but causes a concern to others as the channeler changes. It often takes quite a bit of time for things to come to a new normal state in a household. By all means don't keep things a secret, be open and share your conversations with the family. They will find real joy in giving you questions to ask your guides and then be curious about their guides. Be open about the results and include everyone in the family as they see fit to be involved. The family will test you more than anyone else they will be your most severe critics and your greatest supporters. Once you get your channeling feet on the ground do make them aware of what 'mysterious things' are going on when you are channeling. It will go a long way toward their acceptance of the process and maintaining family cohesiveness.

At any moment of day or night no one does it better than you do for you are your own best friend who has a spiritual family that is concerned with one thing your physical and spiritual well-being.

Chapter 8: The Gift of Gratitude

Leal: Gratitude is so very important. It is an energy unto itself that serves to elevate humankind and light beings, alike. The act of experiencing feelings of gratitude begins in the chest or heart chakra and radiates through the body and out to the energies surrounding the body, causing a resonance as it moves. It is very important that we stop to appreciate all that we have been given, especially when times seem very unsettled and the energy on the planet seems to be coming more and more dense and negative. Now that you have developed an awareness of the support systems that are available to you and have established a consistent method of communication through which you are able to access information and guidance at any moment, you realize you are not alone.

The fear of being alone in your struggles has pushed many of you to places of great darkness and despair. However, there has never been a time in which God's minions were unavailable to you. You do not ever have to be alone again. This realization brings you to the next level of spiritual evolution and prepares you to face the world and all it has to offer with strength and courage.

El-Israel: Gratitude is a gift, but also a responsibility. You have been made aware of your access to assistance, but many others have not. It is important that you appreciate and share your experience with others to assist them in coming to the light and accepting help on their journey. This is the true concept of conversion. We often try to convert others to our way of thinking or religious belief system. In truth, this is not an effective way to bring others to an acceptance of the God within and their own spiritual saving. The concept of taking Jesus into one's heart or acceptance of one's Dharma, or place in life, is rooted in the acceptance of help from Divine sources. This is the concept of listening to the still, small voice, the Holy Spirit. Through acceptance of help and a view to the other side, all people are able to live their lives more fully, in less fear. This reassurance calms the static of the vibration of the planet and all humankind. The goal is for every human to feel the bliss and reassurance that you now experience in the support you receive.

In the years to come we are hoping to see a shift in the value system of humankind.

The goal is to exist peacefully and in loving community with all other people. The way to this is through an understanding that all life is connected and all needs are met through God and the energy of manifestation. The first step to achieving world peace and love is to accept your connection to the Divine and welcome its presence in your awareness. Through the communication system you have established, you are able to ask questions and receive reassurance about your place in this world as it relates to others and the evolution of all of humankind. You will feel peace in your place in the grand scheme of this process; the spiritual evolution of the planet. The acceptance you experience assists you in your growth. For this peace of mind and spirit you will be grateful. The trick here is to not withhold expressions of your gratitude.

It is human nature to be protective of what is ours; to have a sense of lack. Even as small children, growing, we are quick to establish ownership by declaring, "Mine". We understand that if someone takes what we want, it is gone and that there is not an unlimited supply. This is a toddler's perspective that has been carried on to adulthood for many people. The truth is that there is an infinite supply to fill all of our needs available through God. The first step to accessing this supply is through the recalibration of your frequency to one consistent with manifestation of good and abundance in your life. Now that you have established a direct line to your supplier, you may ask that your needs be supplied and the order will be filled. If there is an infinite supply for you, then there is for every other person, as well. You must know this for all others and be willing to share the good news, bringing others closer to God and their source of happiness and love. Spread the word!

Seth: When you hear the angelic choir sing it will move your heart and fill it with such awe that many find their eyes fill with tears. At that moment you have captured the uplifting feeling of gratitude. When you have done a good deed and realize the source of your actions came from understanding God more clearly you are filled with gratitude. Some religions speak of 'Rapture', a concept of the final times, in which mankind (true believers) are lifted into a heavenly state. This elevated state of being is available to all. Through the individual's understanding of gratitude and primarily being a walking example of this state of heart and mind you elevate yourself and all you come in contact with to come closer to your true estate of being, closer to God. As we become an agent of gratitude through our understanding and guidance from the other side we elevate the local vibration of all we come in contact. When you experience the gift of channeling and find that bond between you and your guide your world changes and the whole world takes one tiny step away from the brink of disaster. It is gratitude which radiates and sustains that energy and holds it undiminished and permanently to the world.

As you establish this connection you will become born again, a new person, armed with the word of God. Jesus spoke openly to his Father; you too have an open channel to the greatest source of advice on this planet. Fill your heart, mind and soul, the very fiber of your being with Love and Gratitude and there is no limit to the good which you will accomplish.

Lokar: It is possibly the greatest ongoing challenge of your life to keep your sense of good at this time in earth's history. How difficult it must be for some of you to be positive when there is so much negativity surrounding our daily lives. When you feel down and out, or inundated by current events reach into your heart and radiate your sense of love and gratitude. Don't make it a big deal, just reach inside for it and fan the spark into a flame. Thus armed the negativity dissolves before your enlightened being. Every one of you that chooses to walk this path can know you are contributing to the salvation of yourself, others about you and the planet. Now that's something to be grateful for.

El-Israel: We must consider the issue of expectations, from both our end and yours. You can expect that we will provide you with the most up to date information we have available to us as servants of the will of God. We are able to share with you aspects of your path as written in the Akashic records. It is important to understand that, when your life was planned, many options were "penciled in". That is to say that the possibilities of all optional outcomes for different life choices were accounted for. However, all of the paths lead you back to God and your spirit home. Your life can be very difficult or your lessons can be accompanied by smooth transitions and gentle learning. Having access to your Akashic records, we are able to suggest a path of least resistance and most gain. However, you are always able to choose another way. Our hope is that your suffering is relieved and your spiritual growth and healing be accomplished easily. Having access to this information is something for which you can be truly grateful, as it allows you to navigate your life in the way that best suits you. Remember that you may ask us to investigate other possible paths and their outcomes when you are asking for information and guidance. It never hurts to be aware of a few possibilities and weigh your options.

We expect that you will commune with us frequently; that you will ask for our help and receive input. It is also understood that you will use the information you receive to further your growth and the spiritual evolution of mankind in a positive manner. Consequently, you may ask for financial gain and personal power only if you are willing to use these to benefit mankind. When gifts are received, it is appropriate to give thanks. This can be demonstrated physically by sharing with others and using your gifts to help mankind. The act of sharing is yet another expression of gratitude. Remember that Jesus, "as ye have done to the least of these, ye have done unto me". Giving to others through time, energy, prayer or physical means is also an expression of gratitude.

Seth: The gift of gratitude flows through you to others, but it also flows from us to you. In the grand sense of things there is an unbroken chain which links you directly to the Godhead, the source of all being. This source energizes all through this constant connection of Love and Gratitude. The flow is increased when we connect with you and you with us, sharing the energy of love and gratitude. As you recognize this flow and employ the energy in your daily life it increases all the way up the chain and down again benefiting all. How wonderful it is to be so blessed by God. Your connection to this flow now blesses all you come in contact with and elevates the planet.

Leal: It is so very important to maintain this flow on a moment by moment basis in order to strengthen the connection. For every portion of a second that the energy flow is maintained, great work on raising not only your personal vibration, but also that of the planet and all of mankind, is being accomplished. These are the latter days. This is a pivotal point in the future of mankind and the fulfillment of prophecies. Your devotion to your higher purpose is absolutely critical. You have agreed to come to Earth at this time to assist in preparing the way for all to reach enlightenment and establishing connections that allow for God to live within us all in a tangible and creative way. To be able to experience the love of the Divine for yourself and all other others is truly heaven on Earth and for this you will be grateful for all eternity. Namaste and may you go with the peace of the light of the Supreme in your hearts, minds and actions.

Afterward

Seth: You might ask, "Is this all there is in terms of channeling?" and for some of you it will be. You will continue on with your lives using what you have learned as a resource and guide to enhance what has been divinely given. However, the majority of the readers and practitioners will use this work as a stepping stone. You will be caught up in the energetic changes which this planet is going through. Those of you which seek a more refined connection and greater knowledge of the structure of times to come as well as the workings of the celestial realms, will find them as our team of guides will be sending more information to you through our scribes. Be patient and true to yourself for you will be at the forefront in understanding and preparation for the planetary evolution.

Lokar: It is important to realize this is a beginning for many of you which has been anticipated and yearned for in many different ways. We have not finished with the flow of information and techniques which will enhance your future. We have the greatest respect and admiration for those of you who struggle to move on to help yourselves and others. Bless you all for all your efforts and the good you bring to your planet. We stand united to help.

Leal: It is with love for all mankind, in all dimensions, that we make this information available to you. Our greatest hope is that you reunite with the God within and form an alliance with others who are here for the good of humankind and the planet. Your dear mother Earth is calling to you energetically. An evolution is upon you and, consequently, us all. Even if you do not go beyond the level of introductory connections and communications with your guides and the pure love and energy source available to you through them, the act of regular communion with light beings from the other side will elevate your vibration and that of your fellow Earth inhabitants to the next level. Our wish for you is peace and love for every moment of your earthly life and the rest of eternity in your place in the circle of God. Love to you.

El-Israel: For many of you, this is only a stepping stone to the next level. You have chosen to come here now for the purpose of reuniting the physical energy of mankind with the ethereal energy of the Godhead. Your practice will be regular and each time you connect with your higher self your energy will grow. You will seek out a more involved connection and use this to carry the message to other people. It is through this commitment that mankind can become united in love and harmony. You are the way showers and the beacons of truth that manifest God's love and plan to the world. You are the lighthouse shining in the night and the fire atop the mountain that proclaims the good word of God's plan, absent of fear and frustration, and full of hope for a better tomorrow. May you be blessed in your involvement in whatever capacity you choose to connect with the inner light of your fellow man and the light beings that are here to show you the way. Be the leaders, demonstrated through diligent application of the principles outlined here, and you will achieve a great level of peace and joy. Ask and it shall be given to you. Trust and the way shall be shown. Shalom.

Appendix I: Ready for relaxation

Relaxation

Jerry: The purpose of relaxation is to help you become receptive to a greater degree quickly. These techniques are not exclusive to channeling. They are general techniques which can be employed prior to prayer, meditation or to absolve yourself of the tensions of the day. When a technique such as this is used in preparation to channel it is well to keep in mind that you want to maintain an alert awareness to record or remember the context of the communication. Here are three ways to relax, pick the one that works best for you.

Method 1

Concentrate on your feet, wiggle your toes, rotate your ankles several times and then relax them.

Move your attention up to your calves, contract your muscles and then relax up to your knees.

Move to the thighs, contract and relax. Continue in this way contracting and then relaxing up through the hips, back stomach, and middle torso. Take a deep breath and let it out, then start with your hands tensing and relaxing.

Move from your hands to your wrists and up the arms to the shoulders contracting muscles and using circular motions as you relax. In this process pay particular attention to the shoulders and the neck as we carry a lot of stress and tension there.

Tense the muscles of the face and the front of the neck and chin gently roll your head in a clockwise and then counter clockwise fashion. Feel the tension leave your face from the jaw, cheeks and including the little muscles around the eyes. Tense the muscles release the tension, relax.

Notice a beautiful light at the top of your head, let it come down through your whole body and out through the bottoms of your feet. Be thankful for the peace you now feel.

Method 2

Sit quietly for a moment and pay attention to your body.

Manifest a light at the top of your head and direct it to any place which feels tight, tense or fatigued. Let this light help you relax your body by allowing the light to flow from the specific area of tension down and out the bottoms of the feet.

Repeat as necessary until you fill your whole body with light and let it flow out through the bottoms of your feet taking all tension and fatigue with it.

Vocally, or in thought, affirm that all negative energy leaving you is transmuted into energy that is good for the planet and her organisms. This can be done by simply saying, "transmute" and holding the intention of healing.

Method 3

Whole body relaxation using a count and breathing rhythmically to the count is an effective way to achieve a relaxed state with 10 breaths, quickly.

Start counting to yourself mentally or softly with voice.

Breathe then count or count and then breathe. Each individual will find the most suitable way for themselves.

Say:

Ten, with every breath I become more and more relaxed.

Nine, more and more relaxed.

Eight, with each breath I relax more fully.

Seven, I feel the tension leaving my body.

Six, the tension and stress are leaving my (name the place) leaving it at peace.

Five, I am more deeply relaxed.

Four, my relaxation makes me more aware of my purpose.

Three, the last bits of tension are leaving my body.

Two, I am now completely relaxed.

One, I am at peace and one with my purpose.

Appendix II: Author Biographies

Jerome Filipiec

Accepting things of a non-conventional reality was never a problem to me. I was raised in what my grandparents referred to as a 'free thinker" household. There were no religious biases even though my grandmother could recite the entire Roman Catholic mass in three different languages. Open mindedness was the key, infused with a strong sense of truthfulness and morality.

Even as an only child, primarily raised by my grandparents, life was great. Each Sunday morning was an excursion to a different sight to see. Chicago has 100 plus museums and other attractions. Saturday evening was decision making time as we came to a consensus as to where the next morning's trip would be. My grandfather and I would get on the streetcar or Elevated and spend our morning touring the sight. We covered Mummies to Mums. What I learned from those excursions became gold in later life.

When an early teen, radio was still my link to the outside world, I became fascinated with a single radio program which purported to have found the healing techniques of Jesus. This program left such an impact that I expressed a solemn wish to be able to heal. This asking was to become a foundation stone of my life. For I discovered time and time again to ask was to receive.

I started college in Southern California and received a Teaching certificate in Mathematics and Physical Sciences. Continuing to teach, and getting more education ended with a Masters degree in Mathematics Education and an Administrative Certification. To date I have been in education for over 45 years, working with children and adults. I have taken training from several sources in the art of communication and have professionally worked with large and small groups outside the traditional classroom, but that wasn't all that was happening.

As I kept asking for more and more knowledge, the opportunities to learn and experience came flooding in. Individuals with healing talents, amateurs and professionals, kept coming into my life offering to teach me their methods. My step father, an old soul, made me aware of things such as astral travel and esoteric teachings. After his passing I began to regret all the questions I didn't ask. Thanks to my wife I was introduced to a systematized form of meditation and spent years experiencing levels of consciousness unknown to most through the inspired teachings of a loving Guru.

Today I still take an occasional healing case, teach mathematics at a local college and find myself called upon to participate in this most important part of my mission. It's a wonderful life.

Miriam Stanford–Cusack,

Ph.D.N.H.

As small children, my sister and I would sit opposite each other and send mental messages. I would envision a shell and she would say, "It's an ice cream cone!" All children have this capability but somewhere along the way, most lose it. Raised as a Mormon in my youth, I was told that all people who channeled or communicated with spirits were evil and it was dangerous to have involvement with them. However, in the same faith, we were told to "Listen to the still, small voice of the Holy Ghost." I found this all to be very confusing. I chose to block out messages I was receiving at an early age, as I was unable to control where the message came from or who I was allowing in to my personal spiritual space. I was scared and uneasy, so I turned off my connection and left the church.

My learning focused increasingly on the analytical. I received a B.A. with honors in Biology from The University of Denver, followed by a Master's in Education with a focus on Curriculum and Instruction. In 2012, I completed a Doctoral degree in Natural Health studying the use of frequency in healing.

In my late teens, early twenties, I began to meditate in the Kriya Yoga style. This opened up channels of energy and, over time, I began to realize I had the ability to communicate in a safe manner, with something/ someone greater than myself. I studied Science of Mind and began to realize that I was the creator of my experiences in the world. I began to manifest through creative visualization, positive thoughts and a trust in Source.

In 2002, I was exposed to an energy healing modality called BodyTalk™ and became a practitioner. Through the practice of BodyTalk™, I was able to find a greater balance of use of the left and right hemispheres of my brain; merging my analytical side with the intuitive knowing I possessed even as a child. I began to connect with earthbound spirits and have conversations on a mental level with my own guides and those of the people coming to me for healing. From this a desire to be of further healing assistance evolved and I began my studies in Natural Health.

Eventually, I was able to connect with guides, light beings and angels and express information they gave to me through the use of writing. I became an auto-writer, recording pages of handwritten information for clients. On many occasions, I have been told by my guides in my own sessions, as well as sessions with other light workers, I was to write. It was not until now, that I understood. Now, I am acting as a channel for two light beings, El-Isreal and Leal, auto-writing a book on channeling.

Made in the USA
San Bernardino, CA
23 October 2014